POEMS
2011 - 2021

Poems

2011 - 2021

By Matthew Gasda

SERPENT CLUB PRESS

TABLE OF CONTENTS

The American Sublime [2021]
[Recomposed from 2013 edition, Literary Laundry Press]

1

Each part of the system is just a part of some *other* system that you fold
yourself into: the body into family, family into society—
& so on until it eventually breaks down into the inevitable entropy

of desire when you're only marginally aware of the endless white space
that waits for you at the edge of the fictional landmass of the self—but
these lands, these plates of feeling, are only impressive

because of how they box you in; some moral voices take honey with
lemon: they sing; they plead; they spiral; they deepen; they recede &
return & you & I are astonishingly perceptive in the

ways that the soul can ruin itself alive & something I learned very early
on was how to speak to myself entirely in prayer…as if the evolution
of the self depended entirely on this cajoling & nagging

2

& not on a mindful inattention to birds or flowers or bees or the
dislocated wind that flushes the sky of its reality, & what I fear most is
the scope of death's procedure & what you fear most are

evenings in the country when the sun sets so beautifully that you never
want to stop living & the external world continually mirrors your
internal self-deception until the two are indistinguishable:

the zone of art is the only place where someone can say for sure that
I am here & you are over there, in the sphere of that skull of yours,
thinking about the differential equation of the self, the

prediction or inference that compromises cognition & the integration
of desire is only a way to render solipsism into a feeling & not a single,
awful thought; clearly, in a loose world, the

mind can leap anywhere, be utterly free…because
all afternoon, I've been on the verge of being shot to infinity, at least
since I saw you disassemble the morning into day, but listen:

the human soul (as of yet) remains human so you have to
consider that this kind of suffering is natural; it's not a coincidence that
the thought of death electrifies you with the consciousness of a

crime; & truly, I'd like to disclose my subjectivity so that this anagram
of regular old days at home can stop being such a secret; your whole
life you've been trying to stand within yourself as

a way of having form—illuminating the network of defensive tropes
that make up the small, mystical organism that you have become:
attuned to the naturalness of opiate sunlight or the cells

breaking apart inside of you, starved for energy, copying themselves so
poorly that you begin to age; & when the Sycamore
decides it's time for winter, you have to rake the leaves into the

gutter to be taken away by city ordinance; & in the course of all these
years, you have just been waiting for the mystery to recede
like a wave jerked back by the tide; I wipe my mouth; I wend my

body back into the darkness of yet another rising, making coffee,
looking in the mirror, shaving, taking the dog for a walk, aware that
self-consciousness can only deepen up to a certain

point before you realize that you don't have the strength to get past
the poems that were already in the way & really the mind should be so
bright as to engulf the whole past in its transparency:

its function is improvisational, like sitting at the piano; lately, I've been
in a spiritual freefall, a morning star cast out from heaven, plunging
towards a sea of dead or forgotten radiances, &

my favorite thing is to make tea with rosemary & sage leaves, let it
boil for an hour down to a concentrated cupful heat & taste; these
sensations are more refined in us than any single idea, but

everything is un-deconstructable unless you pierce it through
with imagination: ordinary lives continue: romantic tropes get slagged
off as unnecessary fictions; & only with our concave chests open to

the presence of goodness can we undermine the whole conceptual
framework of nihilism, de-hypnotize the mind, & re-discover the brain
as a soul (pull the rabbit out of the hat)—shimmering:

6

compassion cracks the mind like a bell; truth undeciphers itself like a
song & unlike adulterers, we are simply trying to survive, but
it will swallow us (the light coming in through the

kitchen window), it will turn us into atoms, so I'll repeat: let's
try it again, you & I, with thou; or let's excavate around nothingness &
let the mind find a category for its own dissolution...*please*—

I have fallen through unreal floors, gotten myself enmeshed in
loops of possibility, & only lately have I understood the textual
process of living things; as a rule, I've resisted anything

running contrary to instinct, heart, & reason...because
a soul is just image ensnared in sound, rippling out
infinitely into empty space, so we need to just put up

7

some obstacles so that we may reflect the soul & capture it back in
the center of itself...but the form of the motion is unremembered,
unheard of here & I'm ingested already by the entropy of

home & the inrush of dying all around me; ankle-deep in imaginary
flowers, I'm brought to the edge of my own inner darkening: cloudlets
skirt low over the grass; old men drink

beer to remember who they are, & for a moment I'm released from
the lifelessness & mourning which pushes out from objects & deprives
them of form and idea & leaves them decomposed: a

mass of loosely collected points in space, seeking a life-giving, a
return to form & the endurance of things in the space of the self &
thus, our tropes gently conceal themselves in what comes

8

after: marriage, children, our own sense of unfortunate/fortunate
repetition: the mimicry of real presences, the real emotions that
emerge in the facility of touch, the exchange of childhood memories

through the nerve cells of the hands & the twisting of cognitive
geometry around the immanence of the natural world: the
spreading backwards of sensation in perfect order: homemade

bread & barefoot walks around the block in the middle of the night,
sealing the antimatter of existence together into exquisite
assertions of new, delicate life with no first principles to guide us

only this intrinsic attachment to certain moments,
which we can never link up to the fact that all good things at
one time or another occurred in the present,

9

which seems to exist only so that it can break off into a silver pool of
regret from the growing block of time...so it is better to be jumbled up
than flattened out & perfected because perfection

can never really be achieved except on the smallest scale, so that
perfection demands a million concessions at the quantum level &
leaves us alone with just this: which is a comfort without love or

any other primal anxiety; the stars are spiralling; I'm headed back to
the beginning; it's winter & I'm looking into the fire & you texted me
saying you have a sore throat & that you wish you were

here & there is so much artiface in the good natured circle of our friends & lovers & fuck it: I'm a reservoir of nothingness; I don't know what else to say...Sundays are best—

10

when you begin to move out of your latest ideas, sniff the landscape out, memorize its topology, bring it to a single Archimedean point, which fractures the heart & lets the deepest

illuminations shine through the break at the center of the self, so that all may suddenly proceed onward, without collapsing, sapped by the concept of unity, which can only remind us that we have

none, except maybe for the fragments of what we have of the Greeks, & the music of J.S. Bach, & the personalities of Shakespeare for whom unity or completion did not exist, but was

assumed in the radical music clusters & breaks out of the Mind & connects our loose dreams of each other in a continuum of beautiful phenomena like the fluttering of gold-winged birds,

11

accelerating out of the morning darkness, which is when you most feel the force of love (as if your irises had fingertips & could feel the sudden breakthroughs of form into the heart), which, by the

way, is all poetry is: this isolation of a feeling concealed by the after-image where the wings once were & must come back together again, so that we see something that both is & is not,

which explains why the dead are never really dead in memory, but exist as impressions of themselves in us: fragments of leftover light, which are not really fragments, but points of clarity like spy

glasses or windows to the enchantment of the rain & humid thunder & movies late at night while drinking cheap wine & tea: the secrets to a happiness which comes suddenly

& allows the discrete moments of our lives to assemble into a stream &
flow into the present to form a density of feeling:
an awareness of the heaviness of our bodies (sunburnt & warm

12

to the touch) as if we had passed beyond suffering into a space
uncircumscribed by anything, by a self-consciousness, which is
boundless & ever augmenting, evading a central fixity, which

would mean admitting that life is simple & that all delight &
sweetness vanish in endless turnings inward & self-therapies that
never bring us any closer to some realizable thought or symmetry

of ourselves, having failed to dam up this gradual seeping-out of life,
the fundamental weakness in us, which Socrates called the
daemonic, which philosophy must try to contain, but can never

destroy, as it tears open great swaths of whitened emptiness within
us until we no longer recognize the divine & nature is no longer the
ground of existence, but an isolation: separate from us, ugly,

13

like a shriveled body dead before cremation, linked to a passion for
Being, or the extraordinary flow of emotions, which are always without
any intellectual contradictions at all, like an ant colony in

the crack of a sidewalk, busy, but never confused in purpose, or ever
obscured by time's all-severing wave, always rebuilding life before it is
destroyed, by a child's breath, or the lawn mower, or a

broom, always gathering & rendering a world out of the dust that is
contained in the ants themselves, oscillating like the atoms which make
them up, exceeding the life that has been given to

them, without the fundamental weakness that philosophy seeks to
overcome & communicate in a system or interpretation of reality, or
space, physical & metaphysical (metaphysical only where

the physical fails & has no form): the quiverings & oscillations of
life's primary stuff, laid out against the field of space/time, not space &
time, but the integration of physical movement with the

light from green plants & trees, shimmering around the sun's
centrifuge: there is a pureness & joy lies behind all philosophical
questions "who am I?" "what should I do?" "how does one learn

to die?"—which can dissolve them, like a Wittgensteinian game that
reveals that our problems are only problems when we pose them in
questions, which philosophy speaks to & rationalizes &

tries to overcome—overwhelmed by that of which Plato was so afraid:
the intrusion of Eros upon the integrity of order…as if the mind could
not put into system its own beautiful self-

contradiction, preferring rather, to build pure ideas into forms, which
cannot be sustained—a series of evasions of the indivisible fact of
Being…without the backbone of

logic, or anything: naked (like Lear's vast darkenings & self-denials),
polyps in the otherwise smooth field of space/time, which
philosophy cannot account for & tries to flatten down, unrippling

space/time as if it were a fresh white sheet spread over a hotel room
bed, which will always be ruffled when new guests come & make love
or just sleep because love is a *kenosis* as Bloom says, an

emptying: the inexactitude of the measure of the self, the terrible
widening of space within space, an anti-clarity which is the clarity of
Being-within-oneself, this: physical wavering repetition &

incompleteness, which is not the absence of ideas, but the absence of
real ideas about real things: Olivia in her kitchen with the windows
open & nobody in the house, which we agreed

was lovely in the spring, but so terrible in winter…or Gloria taking out
a copy of *La Rayuela* from her purse to see if I had come there for her,
La Maga—& if I knew that life must be met

with some idea bigger than life, some poetics, which cannot be
reduced, but yet is not some grand edifice of rationality…& ten years
later I barely know what it all means: this configuration of

energy—these dovetailing thoughts, folding out & collapsing upon
themselves, arising out of the subconscious itself: the secret sphere of
the mind, which

often takes the shape of water, which has no beginnings & ends, like
composer's cleft of air…
or the

emptiness which is mirrored in the world, or voice, which is not the
real, but the unreal: an unreal, which is mirrored in Bernini's *Neptune*
or the *Apollo and Daphne* where a kind of suddenness flows

& moves us endlessly, in the potential of the real, or the barriers of the
self, which do not allow us to enclose art & all the manifolds of life
that ripple within the objects of art, & all objects of the senses

not contained within an Idea, or philosophy, the plain systems of
the mind, which try to push language on our images & give them a
firmness, which they cannot have, which they cannot have & still

follow the curve of time, which absorbs us & our definitions in dismal
entropy…but the Mind is healed when the old universal images cycle
through it like chemicals popped into a vein,

attacking a cancer of the blood, which will not quite kill us, but rather
ruin any chance we have of living a normal life or whatever it is called:
this puncturing of images, so that we may see what is

on the other side the meaning of ideas in a conversation at the
supermarket with someone whom I used to play baseball with when I
am suddenly unable to say anything of consequence,

unable to poke a thread of color through the Given, & if you compress
each fragile sliver of time into a poem order emerges from the field of
disorder: dying music and impossible ideals,

incalculable orders of images & sound, held closely in the brain, but
never understood, never pictured in a unity which has no beginnings &
ends—so that it is impossible to understand what

19

the senses are feeling: *that the world is God's exhaustion* & it is absolutely
strange that the mind & the world sync up like this—like
peas in a pod; it's simply hard to accept the post-Copernican

cosmology with the super-abundant consequence of *infiniti modi,* which
deny the Incarnation as something that can only happen once;
there is intuitive evidence, on the contrary, that salvation is a

loaded dice, an on-going freefall of multiplicities—a cascade of maybes
that never lands on its feet—& thus, the stock of
facts is progressively enriched like chicken broth, & the canon of

questions only grows larger like a tumor & in the process of trying to
cope, I've been crippled & maimed by poetry & a few ideas
from Emerson & Shakespeare, so that I'm hunched over in my

20

head like an old man feeding pigeons in a park made of air or
Nabokov bringing note cards to a television interview, afraid of the
patterns outside the self that he could not control or understand,

which assert themselves & attain a shape, full of luminousness without
self consciousness, like a voice that booms from a brainless sky
& we are terrified to realize that we are becoming a total,

indivisible self without any real (necessarily human) feelings that tie
together our past with our present & future, so that we have some
sense of continuity & narrative, not just the continual falling

off of days, like fruit rotting in the grass, returning to the earth without
a shape, without a future other than to become a fruit-bearing tree
again as if we are always certain to become what we

21

always were: unable to ever really talk to each other, even though that
is all we ever want to do, to somehow just see each other in
our total *whatness*—like a sudden burst of summer rain or the light

behind images when we puncture them (always hidden, always aching
to hit the sidewalk & run into the grass), reminding us that happiness
is not a transformation of the object, but the subject—

like a perspective laid flat & rearranged, so that more is captured in
the panorama of thought & feeling & their total reaching out, which is
called revelation: the possibility that something could break

through & corrode all these stone edifices like idols erected on the
island of the self with huge eyes & broken teeth, prepared for an
eternity fixed into place, fixed into the whole structure of the self

22

without any greatness, or what philosophers call the overcoming of
death, when we are full of anxiety, but never quite threatened, as if
death were an insubstantial halo or veil, which we cannot see through

properly & is the reason why we have nothing to say to each other
in the produce aisle... because we cannot see through this tangle of
inessential words & phrases to the innocent fact of our dying, if

not today, then certainly tomorrow... or whenever the point occurs
in space when eternity suddenly stops & we're punctured, as if we've
received a head-wound that lets a new idea in: that we don't need to

step in the traps we lay for ourselves... given that time is always
creating visions & small radiances for us even on the mornings when
we know that we are going to be unhappy just based on the dreams

23

we had the night before, which puncture the equilibrium of existence,
revealing a variegated series of contingencies in this solipsistic
suburban world, so we have just enough rope left to hang

ourselves with: the patterns of people who are like music trapped on
the page (music that no one really has the talent to play) & now I'm
gazing into the camera—can you sense my detachment—?

the underlying mechanics of a normal life are increasingly cruel; & hey,
it takes composure to re-structure a self out of this perpetual mourning
& fix the irregular heartbeat of Being & as a consequence...

the modern looks increasingly like a village where all the old rituals
& dances have stopped working, where people have gone haywire,
trapped in an elliptical, elusive, experimental mode as if

24

living in some primitive darkness before fire, but there's nothing
to stop us from just going on & not in the sense that Beckett meant it
(with courage or moral sincerity), but, rather, in the sense of this dumb

will-to-live however is easiest: without any gaps in the raiment of
comfort & ordinariness while the dental hygienist talks about
bowling in Syracuse, New York where I went to college & how

cold it is up there & how much it snows & all the other minor, but
significant acquiescences to the way people are: like sap locked in the
concentric growing up of days around a life...& what

happens when these punctures heal, when life knits back together like
ivy cut away from a house? can we still have some of the light & air
that comes through like supplies dropped into an encircled

city? because spiritual wounds are like fires in an old, decaying forest
that lets new shoots, new trees, sprout up—tying bundles of memory
together as if they were a piece of music:

Little League games & movies at twilight, first loves, & the novels I
was too young to read while it rained…like the first notes in Wagner's
Tristan and Isolde—tenderly, with all the suddenness of

sight… stretching out from person to person, letting us see with an
almost total vision of love, which roots us like trees into the dirt of
existence & builds up a network of living things

that does not shut off if one of its nodes fails…& if we can all keep
quiet together & let the wounds of speech heal…then we may touch &
see again

with a child-like lucidity & realize that even the pantomimes of
personality contain something which can broaden & receive a light or
even the shadow of a light & grow—as if all human interaction

were just a puncturing & planting in the soil of existence, & maybe
millions or billions of years away consciousness floated out of the giant
molecular pool somehow & became something so fine-

grained & specific that the decomposition of unity & simplicity
happened by accident & we became subjects severed from objects; now
one-foldedness closes into the circle of threefoldedness: the

circular process of self-reference cannot stop hiding from itself, from
the constant, substantial core of material reality: *gravitation, power,
energy…* speaking only evokes sentimental excess,

an over-ripening of the strangeness which endures from the center
to the circumference here in the suburbs: the fictional line that runs
parallel to the daily complaints about a new brand

of coffee through to the seal of fire that divides each one of us from
our essential selves: the energy of obliteration is ecstatic and joyful,
folds you in, parcels you out into nothingness—& at the

point of submerging, a new form is released, & the objects of one
category are transformed into those of another, so the only fictional
ideal today is sorrow for godlessness that we've draped

all over ourselves—parceling out the Imagination into dollops of
cliches & howdyados, holding off the twilight until midday or walking
the dog after dark & no denomination of control or self-

28

satisfaction can make up for an inner loss or vivify the sequence of
myths that have gradually replaced reality in the chain-like
structure of our agape or love because, as you can see, the dog

& the mailman have been playing the same game for years, but neither
of them will ever win in the end & the seamlessness of repetition
with forward motion is astounding: backwards &

forwards—like when I listened to the rain with Gloria in that little
hotel room before I had to go, & sever this chord of new life, cut like a
weed,when I kissed her, hair wet from the rain, matted, &

beautiful, & the train door closed, in a burst of violet-grey & still, the
story of our own redemption comes every day with the newspaper:
how houses are cleaner now or how you can depart

29

from your own emptiness like a bird & in the evening the oxygen
pockets in space break open & catch with fire & that is, after all, the
mysticism of growing old where you were born—harvested

like corn from the graves of eternity (displaced, uprooted, up-gathered)
& here, out of necessity, self-creation takes the place of obedience,
releasing the inwoven pressures of thought & a poem

is a crossroads, a railtown, a port city: a vector of displacements from the scheme of repetition...& because she opened her eyes, my sister must get up, make breakfast, fry the farm eggs, cut the

peaches, drain the yogurt, save the whey for later...& look at the flower-like structure of the universe, how unlike living it really is & couldn't a child tell the difference between the beauty of the

30

Ionian mode & a Sycamore losing its bark? couldn't each metalepsis of poetry last as long as a Hayden quartet? & couldn't each of us begin to replace the ontology of death with a new, more

radiant idea? yes! but the community of poems lacks the materiality necessary to endure: rationality divides people into houses, houses into gathering secrets, secrets into mornings of

precarious self-awareness because an American sublime is not a metaphysical concept: it's an honest perception of movement, color, love: a reworking of autumn finally into frost, of simplicity

into an assertive, fluent truth... even though there's some kind of equation that dictates the rate at which disorder pervades an ordered system & we've developed defenses so complex that no

31

one can get in or out & still the soul still stands open, translucent, enacting a system of self-mirroring out of deconstruction: the color of trees, the emotions of houses, couples stepping out of

isolation to apologize: all these things which are never pictured in a unity which has no beginnings & ends in the giant concentricities of the soul, which ripples & radiates out like the

light that pours through the dogwood leaves, & gathers us in until we struggle out like larvae & uselessly assert our individuality, which is good only insofar as we realize that once attained, it must

be destroyed &...this poem, like a set of lungs,
fills up with air: a climbing wave
of the reconciliation of nature with speech... which begins

32

maybe when we are three or four, before the language games really
begin, & we become knotted up with words, like a first love that
deepens past despair & then becomes something that will always

be dying, but never dead, something that will always be strange, as if
fireflies didn't die in the mornings, but broke apart into pieces of living
light full of the beautiful glooms of summer, middle-aged men mowing

lawns & Phillies games in the twilight on TV: all of these wholly
decent things which have no end, but must end & cannot continue in
perpetual decency & wholeness, like that summer, two years ago, when

Emily would make that almost Russian black bread late at night, & we
would fry it in garlic & olive oil & just talk about where we were while
our parents slept in the house where they have always slept, in the

33

house where, somehow, my imagination found its growth, as if it were
a hearty seed clinging to a barren hill: this simple decency & goodness,
without peculiarities except those which all of us carry around in our

heads, but cannot share, a series of looping equations that never cross
or can be proven to cross, but are only probabilities like whether Emily
will choose, or not choose to make bread, whether the language game

will be won or lost at a given curve & sudden drop in time, as if the
complexity of our garden were mirrored in the house, multiplied in the
same pure, unmappable clarity of this space, the full stream of inner

space, which can never be isolated in its perfect purity: that music
which was torn apart by the Bacchantes a while ago, & occasionally
reassembles itself in one of us, & fills us with sorrow for the Eurydice

we never even knew, but feel, somehow, is everywhere, is always
turning into salt before our eyes, as if Bethlehem were not a series of
storefronts & homes, but a giant resistance in the space of the self,

always unwilling to be assimilated into the system of imagination,
always reserving for itself some unimaginable grief, wave-like in its
rippling & spreading—the muted logic of memory, the meaning of

what memory means: the stream of everything that runs away: sounds
that cannot be arrested: the dog's barking, birds, & the coffeemaker:
sudden illuminations of our being that cannot be repeated though

they always are, in loops & jangles of days & nights which hang from
us, like the colorful materials of an expressionist painter or an Indian
headdress rendered by Durer, & every other literalist of the

imagination, which is never literal... like an archangel's white feathers
as it descends to earth: an assemblage of words, which forms its own
rules that do not say when the game will end, but only that it is

perfectly beautiful.

Memorium

[from 2013 edition, Literary Laundry Press]

To Hart Crane

Enclosed in seams of white, the song's ellipse
Of choral blues and diaphonic waves
Evades the ocean's will, the rhythmic tides,
And brings us to the sea's periphery.

And you comb moons of coral in your hair
With muted flowers plucked beneath the floors
Of sealed stars, suspended in your tides,
And lifted in the tally of your love.

For the scarred ports of death open to you
And wind you into light across the sea...
Of vast white circuits silent in the sound
Of your interwoven many-folded shell.

And in the crossings of our syllables,
I close with you in fragments of the surf...
The flow of all your sea-born voices fuse
Into the imaged echo of your eyes.

Aorist

People grieve because they can't overcome the daily
Household things: the remaining clusters of some red
At the end of November: the abeyance of the un

Reaped darkness in the fields of your palms.
I always said that you were lovelier when you stood up
And took the morning, pressed it to your eyes.

I always saw that you broke through the form you
Wrapped around your shoulders like a shawl, or that you
Could reach out and touch the dead with goodness.

No, it's not the old bitterness again: the tenseless
Verbs that figured your total world: it's only a new
Sound, a new aorist, a new resolve.

The Berlin Letter
(for Gloria)

The sudden lapse of desire for your poems made out
Anamnesis and katharsis. It is all right to conceive of life
In terms of a vast nostalgia as long as it has artistic purpose,
But the world won't permit it unless it is self-supporting.
It's a luxury that even the rich, now, can scarcely afford.
We – we consumptives, mistaken people, workers, die-ers,
We must live, not at your expense, God knows,
But in spite of you, open to life's tragic introspection,
Full of the enormous happiness of people who are
Dying a complete, unmystical death, of people
Who know that they are the only petals that
Have opened, somehow, from being into
The beautiful nonbeing of life.

And again, so close to the summer we met each other
It makes me sad, to think of the woman who was between
Us, and who I never knew. But it is a lovely landscape
And I think of your book and it haunts me.
So beautiful a book. Black tree formations, aspiring
Or despairing. Anyway, that is the way I am.

Salt

The interiors are made of glass,
And the visionary gleam has blackened to the husk.
This mood sustains itself on silence,
Lengthening out like a ripple through
A sea-bird's throat.

You've sanded down the sunlight
Until it is like a grain of salt:
A memory that you scatter listlessly across your
Dreams; a fish-hook in the gut, stars
Falling drunk into the water.

A Poem For Today

The old childhood fears always come
Back to you before sleep, a nothingness
Where you can't see your hands
In front of your face:
The past is elastic
And receptive to your touch; you
Try to mold it into the shape of birdsong,
But it always disintegrates to the music of what
Happened. This house of grief is built out
Of silence and rain and glass,
And the six a.m. light still hangs itself in
Golden loops on the wall. The vowels of the
River in you are clear and
Sweet; they congeal into something like a
Lament. It has never seemed so sad, nor
So beautiful, to be alive as today

The Christian Art

Down to its innermost speck, the un
Consummated spark is burnt, and the ash
Is fed to the beasts of the wild. You
Understand me as someone who is still
Unfinished, who heralds himself with violets:
But even shame is not so strong as the
First most violent poem of the earth:
Of the olive trees and the two-winged
Vessel of your hands. The night is always,
Always a failure. But I will not tell you why.

Upon Entering the World

A reliance on lyricism means that death has entered
You and broken the structure of your tongue...and that
Beauty is everywhere: in the cafés, in the metaphors
Left out to dry on the roof, in the indifferent
Detachment of self from the terror of form.
And your youth leads itself right out of its own redemption
Where it evaporates like a cloud. You are void of the splendor
Necessary to be loved by anyone divine: Your art,
Your secrets are a mimesis of your intrinsic isolation...
Like a last quartet: nerves bundled into a singularity of music.

And The Tribes That Were Before

A Hayden quartet grows so intricate in the
Darkness. You want only to feel the night
Rain as it discloses itself to you on the roof.
It has never been so simple to love as
It is now, in the moments before you fall
Asleep, only to return each morning to dying.
People give off a kind of light like ghosts,
But you've never understood it:
How we can be so strange, so divine.
And we'll have to wait until a new emotion comes,
And preserves our nakedness in salt. When we cry,
We will have realized what we have lost.

Untitled II

You tried to make the night like a poem, folded it
Gently into the ruins of memory.
But the cold has washed you clean of death, and
The breaches of your wounds will not clot with
Your own blood. Our longings stand sealed dark
Within us, bleak against the jawbone of the universe.
The snow falls now like music from the cliffs of the moon,
And all that we have anointed has turned to dust.
Fragments of time are buried in our breasts.

The Man Of Uz
(for Joyce)

What did you cry at me from the top of the stairs?
That you had fallen through the ocean of reality
Down to the floor of stars? That the eyes of
The creature you might have been became unglued
From your tongue and rolled under the door?
Put your thumb here I'll say, taste your own saliva again;
Cross yourself like a whore.
Let me uncross the petals of your thighs and
Let the sun leach away your grace.
Each of us after the violent rain will begin to mimic
Real fear: your own mournful love lacks direction,
It keeps censoring the gentleness of physical control.
If you'd come down here, I'd explain it all again,
Lay you out supine with your arms swimming forward, your
White ankles flashing through Dis, careening, trying
To recover the balance of ecstasy.

Night Swimming

Comb straight through the tangle of deadness,
Mock oranges, and bitter flowers.
Call me inside after the play in the park and buckle me to
The side of the bed. If you crush the skull between
Your teeth, the blood, brains, and imagery will
Swim across the floor. All this is so impersonal,
So much more inhuman than Schubert or religious
Love. The woman on the stairs counts
The dark waves of sleep seething from the room
Above. The bones of the stars will be picked clean
Before we're done.

September: A Year Later

Poetry was the oak trees and the dogwoods
Grown brutal in the dark red of autumn;
Our bodies passed over into faith, our
Skin broken, our blood sloughed on the floor.
We once had a love that could part
Our breastbones, seize us deep
In the heart. But mother, father:
Open-handed, I have lost you, and I no longer
Remember who I was; how rain and snow
And sun could purify me. Someone
Restore me. Someone restore this gift:
The naked birch, our devotion.

The Inverted Fable

There is in you
An old leaven, some black depth which must be appeased.
The blown birds show their whiteness against the clouds:
The reddest flowers bloom, and the rain is slashed with
Oxygen and evening.
Around you there are seasons of blankness as
Of snow, years softening into tunelessness,
Mornings of birth and milk,
Honeysuckle and lily-flowers
growing through the fence.
Nature is busy around us, it brings to fruition the
Phenomenal presence of your living and dying. The twilight
Pours the nightingale's song around you like plaster:
The old erotic secrets are lost and you miss the thriving
Adore which was the *leitmotif* of your average or ordinary day.
To transmit something perfect, to scorn the emptiness
With thunder, this is the resolution of your poetry in exile.
Every enchantment was good: every smell, every shock
Of purity: the instress of lightning in the summer
Crumples you like a paper swan.

Monosyllable

The music drills itself into the soft hollows of sunlight,
Which sticks to your teeth like unhappiness:
You write that you've turned into yourself,
But the meaning is ambiguous even to you.
You just wanted to find a way to say that
You've been hurt, but the language is
Never as strong, nor as bitter, as the punishment
You receive for speaking.

The Music Hall

But there is also this tristitia, an eros too
Violent and transformative to root us in possession.
The piano suites last Sunday glimpsed
Our unhealed existence
Floating in dead spores across the surfeit of negation:
Every day the articles of aesthetic life
Are overwhelmed by the demands of a brutal, human love.
When the beautiful heaviness of childhood is finally over,
You're the one, finally, to bury it behind the shed.

Absence

You read the same page of a novel
Twelve times; his favorite book, you can't
Bear to finish it anymore. The birch
Trees line the road, night-blackened
But shining like husks of dying phosphorus
In the headlights. You
Talk of giants, oceans, stars: nothing
But our own blood will make the dead speak,
And nothing can violate this sorrow,
So terribly have we been joined.
The wipers flick hail-stones onto the road…
There are unsayable things between us, that
We have been left alone. The smell
Of hayfires and the sea. The dark ruin
In our loins. When a child goes
We have only each other.
This is the kind of grief that makes you whole.

Newborn

Everything we've rendered out
Of pain; the mornings in the winter
You closed around me and grit my tongue with song.
Black-eyed like a bird. I only
Wanted to feel some kind of awe at being alive,
To have stood up on fire and dashed myself out
Against the snow.

Assistant Bookkeeper In The City of Lisbon

Your flesh is traced and violated by the moral
Order of inscrutable love: the soul is tacked to the
Head of a ship anchored in the pool of moonlit
Imagery…once you could twine your
Nerve and sinew around the trees, feel their
Enchanted motion. Once the turbulence of form
(Gathering and collapsing out of shape) was something
You accepted rather than used to illustrate the
Numerical mercy of pain.

But the splendor of weather systems and intellectual
Games is now for the eccentric and self-righteous:
Laying naked and limp, you most resemble Jacob
After wrestling with the angel. Two women in
Floral dresses walk down the coast singing hand-in
Hand how it is you knew them. The concentration
And stubbornness of the imagination is
Resistant to the magnitude and order of those heavenly
Women and men. (The plume of a wave is a gloss on form.)
And you thought you had a single soul.

To Feign Is To Love

Tonight, I bathe you in water and vinegar; I comb
Through your hair with honey and salt. This hunk of
Bread is not flesh, but imagination teaming with
Ferment. What erotic renewal is has something to do
With innocence and metaphysical, Hellenic girls.
So the earth is reused over and over until it is
Threadbare and wasted. So you find the feminine
Nerve, bundle it into an ignoble ark.

Winter Morning I

Birds must dip their plumes in space:
We are the loveliest in the dark,
When the moon sews itself up between the trees.
Morning is a kind of flood that gurgles
Out of us. It is a hymn we sing to Eros,
A curve we trace in light.
And winter has deprived us of memory. Our
Natural life ripped from us. Now we are
Sustained with stranger, more beautiful things.

Monocacy Creek After The Storm

The deepest noons, the solitude of suburban houses,
The illness of relatives: you are yourself the relation between
Consciousness and language, the copula of the existence around
You and the water, which has assumed the
Incommensurable presence of art. As you walk, you curve towards
A poem like a star pulled towards a tear in space.
The numinousness has never been here except when
Derived it from the wholeness of a terrible, physical love.
You will proceed then: you will throw the stone of
Silence through the sky.

God's Acre

And this is how you make it sacred again,
The way you tune an instrument,
The way you pray to nature to let you feel anger again.
Remove the skin from the rotting fruit, wrap
The new self around the kernel of the new ritual:
The receiving of death and desire in your hands.
Look overhead; a thundershower hangs upon a tree.
Look Endless; how the antipodes pulled you apart.
Everywhere, I'll hurry you into form.

In The Year Of 13 Moons

The suffering that is a presence in you
Is the space of a world without a star
(Or the freedom of aloneness and desire).
Violence is a strange, immensely human act:
It is within you as much as love.
To rise then, with the ungolden dead, to swim
Back into the uncreated: this is the idealism
Of your nature: this inner-motion of prayer.
Outside, the trees are noiseless in winter.
You strip yourself of other people, their sharp,
Sterile glitter, like salt.

The End

You listen to Bach's *Cantata 51*, the second
Aria, and you lie in the sun and
The sacred is everywhere.
The echo of this music is like a child in
You, or a flower...and to touch you now
Would be like mourning: the
Hoop of darkness opens before you
And the teeth are like angels.
Grace is giving your love to the earth,
Flinging it like seed across the waste.

Memorium
(For Iris)

Each day is a failure to speak
what is inside of you. How
gentle winter is. How each morning

seems frail, at the point
of breaking. Life and death are
merged at the root of them,

the all-white trees: the sacred
you are only beginning to
understand (why we must surface

again and again out of
this ocean of loss). The walls of
the Memorium are made of glass,

and you can see the dead above
you. If you could only hear them speak,
you could believe in them again.

Blue

This tangle of beauty, like a Greek vowel,
Made concrete in your devotion to spring:
The house where you were born receives shadow
And sunlight like oil through its pores. And every day,
Your grandfather dies just
Around the corner, the way he always has.
It will be years before you understand
How it was miraculous to have lived here, to have
Been moved to mercy by fear.

Two Novels

1.

It only seems obvious now that we must structure
Our metaphors around the semantics of wind, or
The crying of saplings, broken against the rain.
It has never been shameful to breathe, to winnow
Oneself down to a single, ringing column of light, or
To have come through with our annunciations
More like prayer than sorrow.

2.

Mornings are impenetrable like the keyhole in the throat:
I am taking the world as I found it. I am bending it to you
Like the marrow that pours in from our environs.

A Voice As Of The Waters
(for Emily)

I moulded you. Spread the oak leaves of childhood
Across your chest, heaving under my hand,
Your tongue stilled, the marrow of your heart
Still yellow, your whole being heavy with
The narrowness of dying.
Brother, I hear the wind. Brother, I hear the last
Crickets of August and the long spears of grass
Pushing through your teeth.
You, my other, are so homely and rude:
A butterfly brooding, a helping of sunshine
In the lap of the afternoon.

Spring Wakens Too

Our gatherings nowadays
Are more and more sentimental, and
The creature you were has penetrated far into the body
Of the creature you have become. Every hour
Of radiance in summer is equal to
A well-painted almond blossom, and each
Voice of the as-before enters the circle
Around your head. Out of the kitchen door you follow the
Ash path into the evening, and the bell-voiced
Children play next door until after dusk.
(Poet: the nettles in your tea are for innocence and
The rind of the tangerine is shucked off
For pleasure

Phidias

Even poetry and sculpture are no good for the
Soul turned towards the archetype of desire. You
Make an inner-gesture and yet nobody stirs:
It is extraordinary how we find joy for music and
Endurance, how the mouth and palate strain the vowels
Of sex away so that only the hymn of flesh
Remains. You are a flood, singular, disembodied
From its own source. In the wilderness of premature
Grief only the stones and trees survive this
Prodigy of gloaming. Words and singers will
Crumple back into some epiphanic darkness. A
Desire at the center of cognition whitens for
A pinstripe of faith. As a child you suffered in the
Endless beginning of a life; as a lover you suffered
In a house without wine and secrets. Tread down
The feeble daffodils; run along the train-tracks
In the snow. Deliver me, my love, from this elegy of
Presence.

Our Idle King

I wouldn't say that before the ash compiled its
Dreams we were any more punched through with
Emptiness than now, only that the terrain of
The body hauling itself out of the night
Has changed itself for good. Look: the blueberries are
Bleeding and the ground has been rubbed down to fire.
So you bumped into me, you traded your assemblage of
Colors for nothing. The longing of the body is to
Stand outside itself, to pull out the pin holding the weave
Of consciousness together. When your ears stop ringing,
The noise of silence will surround you like a bell.

Donald At His Sixtieth

When a father buys his son a black tie he means
That he'll need it enough in the years to come. At the
Center of a life is a boundary line that tells you
On which side of the dead to stand, and straddling that
Single, luminous point, one feels how limited the
Space is on one side, and how unlimited it is on the
Other. Further and further we always seem to get
From ourselves, from the daily history that tells us
Who we are. The flesh of the intellect cannot seem
To grasp that our neurosis is not a disorder, but a wound;
That a family forswears itself in forgetting that its
Inwardness is not a gift, but an implicit faith
In the comprehensive spirit of the ever-meticulous
Middle-class. The tie a father buys, yes, the one
He loops around his son: that it is the kind of hymn
That makes it out of the church into the everyday:
That's an instance of devotion and admiration
So improbable that we forget that it's the only
Reason that fathers and sons have to love each other
At all. (And do you remember how the living-room
Furniture had a strange, emotional gravity,
Like all the household objects did? It's as if the furniture was
Imbued with what we were always failing to notice
As it built itself up and collapsed around us
Like a house of cards.)

Waking Up From Art

It would be better to shield the inner self than watch
It collapse under the bright arc of the sublime.
At the symbolic level, cognition is plumed with rose
And pearl, glittering like salt as it dries on the skin.
You want the same fulfillment as other people, the same
Relentless contact with human form. The delicate adept
Sings at the last step of the sea. What the body does
When it faces annihilation is a miracle because it loves.

Summertime

The walk we took around the block last night: when it was strangely cold for August, and we agreed how beautiful home is and how we have woven our childhood into the latticework of the stars (and how frail memory is, like glass). Every night, we are just waiting for rain to fall from the twilight, the air to cover us with regret. Clusters of white lilacs fall like the voids within you. (And we know that we are separate from the love we feel.) And you tell me that this is a golden age.

Stone Harbor

Now what strength is...is the the limitless defiance of
The untroped world. In the houses just over the dunes, light
After light moulds itself to the wind sweeping over the beach
Like a twelve-tone mass, and your
Delicate, flowering body obtains its own musical structure.
In you, the central cognate is hacked, and the wound of
Silence shocks you with its abstraction.
The quiet of everything will not leave you;
It will not trace its way back into prayer.

Autumn, Again: Part I [2014]

1
the blurred violence of the
countryside
untranslated from what it was:
an aphoristic
photograph
bleak flowers
bleak water
(the erasure of a fallen
tree)

2
lightning buried
in the hills:
poetry must pass through the flesh like that
(like light through a vacuum)

3
the Mind darkening
windless &
the light
of the Indian summer
unseen at the center of a
red sky
so cold
so clearcut

4
our hymns are no longer vocable
they are pure Voice &
how almost imperceptibly the oak & the elm leaves
hang like pearls from the
collarbone of heaven &
how when you began to speak to me like that I
begged for you to never stop
& you didn't

5
a single red grain persists in the void
of Time
which is
distributed evenly across the
indifferent soul
making a pattern like a bell-curve
or
like a fugue ringing in the ears
or
like a noise in the sea
crying out in anger

6
from the foam of nonexistence:
the eternity you came from is the eternity you
are going to
& many billions of stars (like people) shamelessly
starve for oxygen (you think)

7
our faces look like wallpaper flowers frozen in a
state of bloom
because you've cured
yourself with a glass of garlic & dandelion juice
& now your skin looks red & healthy exposed
to the sound of light

8
& we shouldn't fear what we don't understand
(being born into life) &
we converge
in a single Abstraction
like two awful blooms falling
from NOWHERE into
a still pool of water

9
our light will pass
through the
leaves
like
a hand
through water

10
so describe the dance-like movement of
your inner-light
as it slides from one end of the room to the other
in
the course of these afternoons
together
(because absence
is a form of radiance
you know)

11
rising through
the depths of the grass we don't encounter any
resistance on our way to becoming Total
& what we have
(what we can count on)
are small things like
moons & fishes
& Chinese-lanterns
& the sense that these things are
too precious to retain a
place inside a poem
& we could try to bring the Overall to a single
point
(but something lost there
is irretrievable)

12
a star
dying in your palms
like a bird
with a broken wing
sheds no light

13
& the Overall shuttling across the sky looks like a
giant traipsing
across a meadow &

if you want access to the ideas inside these hail-
stones you have to open them with both hands

14
because everywhere we are surrounded by linkages
&
dissolutions & images
& because a poem welcomes us
into the Open
(line: integration:
a structure of incommunicable enchantment)

15
mothers talking to children & children talking in
the voices of birds & birds talking in the voices
of angels & the transformation is never pleasing
when it occurs without our awareness of it & the
scaffolding of music is the first to collapse inside
the ear (& that's why our ears are always ringing:
because annihilation is always forgotten when we
speak from the inside)
& subject
& object
could emerge
from the
radius of the same circle
(if they wanted to)

16
a projection of some
other Voice verging on
the sacred
& the destruction of the trees signals
the end of
the life-&-death
cycle

(because
there are many renewals
contained within
a single renewal)

17
a bare house
stripped of its
mental furnishings:
a blue house
built inside an autumn star

18
pieces of sound are
falling
while
you
stand there
with your mouth open

19
our mourning is as quick as lightning to strike us &
the Mind is a healing process as much as it's a
mental process & the concussion of the
Unknown gathering inside the Known is terrifying
like a blue artillery shell
brightening over a trench
& the burden of energy is its spiritual irreducibility

(the tendency to manifest itself
as a visual abstraction)

& we must exhaust the outpouring of
this Source
at Its source
so we don't
betray the realization
that we are the only ones who can

20
& we (children of the stars)
are always mirroring
the Kosmos
& a paper moon
can be folded
back into a swan
if you can trace
the geometry of pain

21
cultivate a
responsiveness
towards love:

because
what we're feeling is
the zero-gravity of tumbling off the horizon of
time:

22
factors of thinking emerge to assert themselves as
True in the
vacuum of
self-realization & a fifth
can become a third as quickly as a symphony
can become a string quartet

23
this earth is as unstable as our being together
& to swallow a cloud would
be a miracle
& so would waking up to an eternity of happiness
or something like it

24
shedding ourselves of the summer & its intentions
& a
radiance is a radiance is a radiance
(& we would garner no attention
from the sky if we disappeared forever)

25
so believe me when I say our features are wholly
human for a reason
& are meant to be
symbols of
winter
& its absolution
& the cognitive
firmament is as transparent as
time is
& our miraculous self-love is not the result of any
substantial
meditation but just is & is not
more hysterical than our being here
& the more mystical the Mind gets the
more unclear
it is
as to what
It is

26
every unveiling

of autumn light is the unveiling of something in-
conceivable about the vacancy of the afterlife

& this is
not chaos but this is not order either & halfway
between limitation & limitlessness is where
you become shocked at your own serenity
&
the trees glow blue today
dying
the way they always do
this late into October

27
& the question of love is always
asked the same way everywhere
& the murmur of love is always explained as the
same
irrational
beginning of a mystery
beginning with an "I"

28
we have to insist on being ourselves
&
watching the
lightning strike down around the yard
I realize that the hush of the all-beautiful is the
hush of being alive
& look!

29
the last green trees
are holding onto their
integration with pride
& speak
o' Unspoken-For
& lean
through the invisible presence of the sun & feel
its joy
& know that the
autumn is for You
& that it breathes like
You do
(just the same)

30
we are protected by a shield of lyricism
& a trace of heaven
flashes before your unclosed
eyes

31
the leaves fall
like patterns of water around you (constellations
flowing overhead)
& you will never be
meaningless as long as you stay
where you are
(which is alone within yourself)

32
the foxgloves are boxing
us
in
so why don't we clip them
finally
& put them in a jar?

33
a way of finalizing sorrow &
making motion out of stasis &
we can locate everything wrong with
us in our failure to attain pleasure

so listen again to the wind & assure me that forget-
ting is the best method of rotation

34
now from major to minor key:

open the Soul &
edify me
dear
(shake identity off like rain from a raincoat)

sustain me with your
hunger & bare necessity
& explain to me again

what we are
evolving into?
is it grace?
is it the grass
we clipped
& stacked
next to the driveway?

because
consciousness has its own
Shakespearean
way of talking to itself
just like we have our own way
of talking to
the stars

35
our way of perceiving
is an emotional mode
& we are like two mariners
on a flat-bottomed boat exploring
a moonlit sea
& this is the final
& the first Crossing
at the same time
& the shadows we

etch in the soul are no more earnest than our sand-
castles are
& we have always said we feel guilty for living
indoors but don't mean it

because the weather will always attack the foundations

of the house to punish us
(so we wait & wait & wait
for it)

36
& now autumn
gives way
(finally)
to the winter
so take this
November orchid
(unsewn)
& place it back in
the burial of the spring
& let's try again with endurance
(let's try to soothe the
Dryad weeping for
its lost seed)

37
I want you to
experience humility for once
because that's what I want to do for you (help you
be humble)
& don't circle around an old broken
god & laugh
or stand up at supper &
walk out of the house
because who are we to say that
we stand inside a different
church of self-survival than
everyone else does?
(or that when the
sun rises
we are the
only ones shining?)

38
selfslaughter
is a spiritual vocation
& your sense of the
numinous
has always moved me
Darling
& I know
that it's a part of me when
I enter the room
of discredited silence
(as a ritual) & shift
the furniture around to seem as if
I've really
been living here

39
the weather is incoherent
& the moon is lost
& we
still have a few secrets left
& this alone makes us Good
& the spirit will punish
what has already been redeemed
because the spirit knows
that discipline is an Art

40
tell me Poet: do you see the
blank inside?
can you see the redness glowing through the frame
of the leaves?
(because
like
Emerson said
writing in his journals:
trust
that what is there
is there)

41
a displaced feeling that
pain is our life

so: change the question
so change the answer
so change
the contemporary mystical framework of techno-
logical pleasure
(the association of Truth
with dissolution
& disassociation)

42
constantly & radically disappointed by the infinity that
passes through us like
a wave of sound
or
a wave of water
& our opening-up is everything isn't it? to the
world
& everything
(letting the soul fall over
the autumn morning
like a shadow
over the lawn)

43
the days passing like jesters
in a deck of cards
& why are we so content to watch them pass
(the days & the suns)

?

& what about the
faded woman
next door
who is always crying
about lost love

as if she were a girl of sixteen covered
in enough lace & fragrance
to fill a room

?

44
&
it's not innocence I'm talking about
it's that inexhaustible
trace of cognitive emotion
&
what
I see of you is what you see
of me

(how the earth moves
around us
& how touch loses
its violence near the point of
absolute discretion)

expressions coined for the purpose of talking about
autumn
again
& it's raining
again
& will you speak
to the eternal
that grows &
dies
inside of each
of us
like a rose?

because as of yet

there are three modes for
saying something other than
what one means:
but all modes
are primarily ontological when
spoken as poetry
& shameless
aren't you?
my Flower-Of-The-Valley:

& death is a searchlight
& we are searchlights in a cold universe
& that mournful song of yours is the one you sing
to yourself
& boy o' boy is it a thirst or what?

(this strange wanting
of nothing but pure
emotional love)

45
we are self-trained in a private
language
of deep
almost unforgivable
tautology
(& if your summer teeth fall out
who will sweep them up from the floor?)

& pass a piece of sunlight through your fingers let it
break off like a piece of the moon
or like a sorb-apple from its
branch

& tell me again what we're here for &
tell me again & then
sing it for me
Child
because after a long illness you can
sing anything you like
& you can
return
to consciousness like a
dancer entering
the spotlight
from just offstage

46
remember our letters & the wingbeat of their
laughter?
because it's impossible to come down from this
kind of dreaming

& you are always telling me
that compassionate
people are suffering people
(& they really are)

47
screen our movement
with light

betray an intuition
heal us with a cut down
through the eyes:
cut
stare:
a new
more
translucent
way of seeing:

your beautiful unspoiled
hands
opening my
eyes

48
a lantern swings through a
field of darkness
like a page in Emerson's
journals
turning itself
over in the Mind

49
Paraclete
you have
a sweetness
that
for me
is like
piano music

50
& remember Mozart's death
in a pauper's grave? (the
Roman jonquils & anemones
in his hair?)

51
seeds of unfallen rain
so delicate before the dawn
& say:

'bleached water
wash me clean of this
spiritual deadness
take this layer
of human skin
away'

CODA

close
the eyes of the
bitter moon
above you

because
I
& all the others
will love you
my
Eveningblue

(I
&
all the others)

Autumn, Again: Part II [2017/2021]

1
dreams
like nettles taking over
the garden

2
there is a gap in today
that you
must fill with
emptiness
undistributed from the past:

the contradictory &
complicated imagery
of being your mother's
child

3
spring
coiled within
our language
like the spring
inside
the seasons

4
the small wind darts like a soul
&
birdsong comes &
goes all
day long

5
we
bury
our
poets
with
stones

6
because tropes
that fire
together wire
together

7
a nuanced
form capable of
bearing the immense
weight of
the heart

8
because devotion in a
notebook is not the same as
devotion in life

9
the dead edges of perception
peeled off like skin & what I'm trying to
say is that I regret so many things, but
not *this*

10
the natural world
is a metonym for
the human body,

11
but the human body
also operates
within the framework
of the natural world

12
because:

theology is an instrument of vision

(presence withdrawn
into the guise of absence)

13
ballet shoes
like molted feathers

you were the dancer
I stripped like a chambermaid

& everything is brutal when
unthought of

14
& you
become less fragile
open to
indeterminacy & experiment
(I clasped
your hands without loving you
completely)

15
constellations of metaphor
scattered across the mind's dark

(at the bottom
of consciousness
there is another
consciousness
which *knows*)

16
grown fat
like a gourd

in the Indian
summer

17
mass the nettles into ruin
make tea
& wait & wait & wait
your fingers
sobbing like a mourner's

18
what uprooted is

rearranged:

you are not innocent
injured
or weak
I have to say

(regret
faces back at you like a
dog at the door)

19
Shakespearean music
or
pressure where the hurt was a universe

20
grief-strained like whey: trans
parent & full of what once
was
light

21
hands bloodied
like the
color of hibiscus flower
steeped in a clear jar

22
because
vivisected eyes
mourn
the heart
they endure

23
what holds together the lusters in a poem?

the lexicography of words
we appended to nights
of untallied
embryonic stars

24
the ten dimensions
of string theory:
the structure
of falling asleep

(silhouettes
close to the surface
of last year's
dreams)

25
name: theory: belief: attribute:

a separate formation links
a sign to the heart

26
crept down the embankment

found your fingers

creeping through the grass

unnoticed
amidst
the falling sparks of soapy rain

27
an interior membrane that responds
to touch:

a threshold clustering
at the threshold of sight

28
a process of discovery is
a closed circle

29
like an observation plane swooping
through the emotional weather

30
write to haunt (it's the only way
you know how)

& did you forget the feline sun

before it buried you in sleep?

31
we ought follow the
structures of
memory
like music

32
a well-known logical conundrum
postulates that our own universe is only a
nanosecond old

33
I formed
you over
lament

drew you as
a wave
teased you

into a loop
pulled you out
of time

34
Daphnis choking Chloe
twisted
in the dirt
like the shadow of passion:

summer's exhausted
broken-glass love

35
essentialize an
unalterable
view of the brain:

follow the spiral
which curves
inside of

the
future tense

then
structure the soul

out of distance

36
the sun rotting
in the grass
like the body of a bird

37
children braid
their hair with stars:

a nameless one disowns
this offence

38
the heart emits a vacuum
when you seal it with disappointment

39
devastation is for
brighter angels
signaling along the
highway for a lift

40
herbs bolting
too bitter now for
anything except
peasant's tea

41
intricate un-death
or autopoeisis in-
distinguishable from your
beginnings
or the poetry
you trim from your brain

42
cold winter day
Father stacking
firewood outside

every November has been like this
for years
moving in no direction all at once

43
cut the body
down from its splendor
like a corpse from
the scaffold

44
since our life is mapped by the zodiac
this all makes sense

dagger in hand
eyes on the stars

45
archetypal &
anterior to all but himself
alone

re-organizing & self-organizing & according

46
to this representational schema

the world is fleeting
& you
are nothing

47
eyes open &
teeth dead set
against
dreaming
for too long
I
arrange my own thoughts into a trajectory
that only you can follow

48
old thoughts
begging for
new sounds

49
metaphors
enjambed
in the door

50
grieving for the person
you were

51
a fallen world
sunk
like
wagon-wheels
in the mud

52
clear away

lost
beginnings

lost symbols

let the brush fire work its way
through the hills of Becoming

53
between
mourning &
melody
something
we call
'emergence'

54
a circle deep
in the brain where
no one is betrayed

55
a
mimetic shadow

a
sheet of glass about to be

punched through

56
the
torn-up anti-
matter of the
ghostself

57
place your faiths like seeds

58
you cut earthskin with
a pocket-knife
& the rain falls to cleanse the wound
you made

59
the great symbol of Death
on the cross:
so close
to the heart of things

60
everything is
asked of us

but *this*

now & then

(now & then)

Orchid Elegy
[2017 Sagging Meniscus Press]

1 Petals like
characters in a play.

2 Healing the body away:
like the revisions of the early Schumann
by the late Schumann.

3 Exposed nerve of the
crushed flower—cut
into light.

4 Frozen like a songbird
caught dead in winter:
let go of nothing that
does not heal.

5 'I hold the river of
you upon my eyelids
when I cannot sleep.'

6 Now a black sound falling
from the atmosphere: rain
on the drum of the earth.

7 It was along the secret
of your skin: flower-rooted whiteankled Eurydice,
spinning back into smoke.

8 Like a mobius strip or
whatever you were: jointed between
words, twisting
around the poignancy of grief.

9 Your skin thrown over
a delicate muscle (flower
of Eleusis, barley seed,
unformed stem): 'so lift the trees
& raise the dead.'

10 Like eyes foaming
under cold water: petals,
poor as nature, pressed
against themselves
in the cold.

11 Turn back the bookpetals,
chalkwhite, like the sails
of a Greek ship lost in a
vacuum of stars they
call the Kosmos.

12 Replete in your shell, dishevelled
with life: an earthenware
jar placed at the threshold of silence.

13 Dislocated & bent back
together: because so
much is uncertain
when spring vanishes
like a dancer
from the ballroom.

14 Sanatorium glass: internalized
in the mind—this
is what you look through
(a lacerated sadness).

15 Because poems without names
still long to be touched.

16 A bloom like hands
drawn away from the face.

17 & so
you broke
the bones of the heart.

18 Flowing north, like
iron in a bowl of water:
aiming to find the world that is.

19 Your pollen
grains held together
by a glue-like alkaloid:
rudely formed, blue as a
cornflower's.

20 Yet it was the rain
that was torn
to pieces by the shape
of the light.

21 Demeter-lure
(*physis*,
lost-one),
sorrowing mother—
searching for traces of
frost
on the grass.

22 Then your muscles tense
& release like an infant's
hand around its mother's finger.

23 & if it were not
for the silhouettes I
see of you I
would designate you
as no one (a lonely
moon pulling at
our tides).

24 A noise
made
in the slashing open
of your music.

25 The ghost of a mental
flower: ankles
turned, ligaments
hurt: calyx-mouth
open like the obscure
metaphor of pain.

26 Self-sustaining, far
from the sea, like
a little radio play:
& slowly the
poem emerges from
its secret.

27 Tipsy nerves
curving along
the center
of your stem:
quietly fading
towards the resemblance
of a name.

28 Fireflies
sweeping
across
the river
outside &
there is no
biological
grammar
which accounts
for the cinema
inside of thinking.

29 The petals of her eyes
floating up like drowned
ships suspended inside
of poetic loss: 'because
the wound is the place
where the light enters you.'

30 Like a bird at sea
answering through
a circle in the ear,
or a dress, open
at the waist.

31 Having fulfilled in
you nothing which I
was looking for (& everything
which I was).

32 I placed my hands on
your ribs,
breathed through your
lungs: tasted the flesh of poetry
between your teeth, touched
the bright Narcissi
in your hair.

33 A figure or face, shedding gravity
like water—we
dare not cross the almost
Orphic protection
which surrounds you.

34 Like petals which
touch lovingly
as they remember themselves.

35 Where the moon strikes
the throat's tissue: evoked
in the bare, radiant
manifestation of a signature
beyond all context.

36 Out of the slender
emptiness
like a swaying lover, girted
round by night.

37 The brain is
silent: a snow of
neurons falls over
a map of everything
we've lost.

38 You were dislocated
from the earth during a
flowerless spring &
we were unused to
hearing such emotion
in your voice.

39 So everything is carried away: ritual-tree,
Bodi-tree—& we
are bound in a strange
night: never closer,
never free.

40 Poems made of orchidpetals (& the most
important category
of beauty is the beauty
of that which is lost).

41 Memory's
translucent
sheath around
the blackened
flower of the
heart.

42 Petal-like around
the single pistil: an
aporia of the present.

43 Self-enclosed on
open terrain: listening
to the acoustics of
disavowed need.

44 You wade
towards the spring perpetually spiraling &
almost dead, beautiful Orpheus
laying there on the banks
of the river.

45 Water is your metafigure: folded
along the convex
of your shell.

46 I gave you teeth:
fitted them
to your hands—
to the fragments of the earth
we are made of.

47 Accomplishing a
repression of every
instinct of grief (because
words have no other
meaning for us).

48 'I'll collect stars
in a wooden bowl: scatter
your petals overtop the
light, watch them
clot like proteins in
soured milk.'

49 Opening like a
moonrise in reverse:
your eyes close
against me.

50 Foundling
language—
silo for capturing
the future—
pearl-pale,
leaves not
wider than a
knife-back.

51 'So an Odysseus is
always charting the stars
finding his way back home—despite
himself.'

52 A semantics joined
at the navel of speech, a braid
of grammars inside the poem
(& things which matter most
should never be at the mercy of
the things which matter least).

53 Chora: poem of a place,
desert of a desert—emptied of itself.

54 Despite nothing, I'll
scrape a fable from your skin.

55 Like unburying a
body, you would float
towards the world like
a lost balloon.

56 As fragile as body in a
dissection room, or an Orpheus
spinning on his
heels: a devotion which
does nothing but forgive.

57 Growing at a right angle
to the axis of the root & the
analogy extends: deconstructs
the surface of your skin.

58 A sort of cinematic music
from which the action
unfurls along
the spire of the cathedral (which
plays the role
of a radio antenna): 'because
you love the formless:
the radiant zigzag
becoming.'

59 A glass Orchid
pressed between the
paper of a book: I could not
love in the company
of another.

60 So much like
the lie the curtain
makes when it closes
on the play (& the flowers
of some species supposedly
resemble moths in flight).

61 &
when you shut your lens,
you
begin to see a role
for blindness
in the scaffolding of sight.

62 & so often our dreams
have no explosion or catharsis: no
beginning or end (it's kairos: an opening
weaving braiding
flower of thought
(& metanoia: the sewing of regret)).

63 A theology of embodied
time (the act of
seeding as grieving)—the undelivered
wound of memory.

64 These dreams in a rainstorm, blind
even unto
unknowingness (askesis:
the logical space of the flower).

65 Objects without verbs
like marble stars
strewn across the floor.

66 Mercy
remembered
in the sunlight
of the mirror.

67 Fractures
earmarked like reread letters: a tenseless voice
voiced
for falling time.

68 The tide rose
over the cathedral,
flowering in the mud.

69 Emergent, radiant,
like mass to matter, concealed
in the search for
names: you failed again &
again to ask
for what you wanted.

70 Decomposed
fires were swept
from this long
sleep without scars.

71 Phonic lesion, a dislocation
inside the ear—melodies repeat,
cross-referenced in time.

72 Unthreaded spindles laid
on the kitchen table, the
stars spilling out like
grain from a sack.

73 I measured the stripe
around your thighs, washed
you clean like a voyeur
with photographs & letters—
brought you to this permanent
domain of dreamloss
(singing like at a burial).

74 To convey the elasticity
of anguish in cinema: muting
all the images that
do not touch or breath.

75 A soul which surrenders
like a circus animal
under the lights.

76 Thresholds
cluster
at the threshold of
sight.

77 It is incised in the
cortex at the moment
of birth: the data of selfbewilderment (like a blind
drawn
down across
the street).

78 It stunts between the voids of the
body, drives itself
under the surface of the
beloved: open to the needing
self (closed to what
is feeling).

79 A silence is held back
& released in a
swarm (& I am
for this all-engulfing
hunger).

80 What appears
in the form of tropes
shifts: dilates:
bends
around the general
grammar
of the heart.

81 & you are asleep
in a very real sense: shorn
of persons, gripping
tight to a mountain
of abstraction.

82 You grow where death
perforates
the scaffolding of beauty.

83 'You laid them in
the sound of place
& they heard you.'

84 Coronal blood, a
sun slipped
under the door.

85 When the cranes
are folded back into paper, flesh
& feathers are left on the floor.

86 A sacrifice in Sanskrit charged
with the conjugated verbs of a lost infinity (a
wheel without spokes: a memory
turning in the place
where the poem never was).

87 I baited the stars
on fishing-line & cast
them back into
the water:

88 A thematized
closeness, like
the fractal
of a season
(spring without
spring, dreams
without days).

89 You were a figure danced
into porcelain &
you heard without
listening where
the memory was
in the picture-heart.

90 Eleusine grain
fallen into fire, gathered
back as loss.

91 This is the slender organism
from which radiates all the other
planes of the body: a skeleton
grafted inside the skin.

92 '& you imagine that it's
an easy thing, but it's not
an easy thing—to make
a world up.'

93 The stars laid out
like bodies in the grass: so
offer me language like sleep (give
rain or take it).

94 Everything is
folded into the
text, because the soul is
always beautiful when
unreceived.

95 An inwoven pressure
tinged with radiance, suppurated
from the bone
of self-possession: &
what is the color
of what is essentially shimmering?

96 'Because we
feel ashamed
when the dead
return.'

97 Petals, like
soldiers crossing
& uncrossing
the Marne.

98 I traced love
across the surface of
singing—& I saw you,
hearing me.

99 & you were
undestroyed,
like water.

100 Birds split open
at the throat: the
silver bulbs of the
music stolen.

101 Intention drawn
from the shell
of hollow pearl you
called agape—
the scarred, tissue
of the brain & mouth.

102 I'll dismember the
other flowers, knead them
back into your flesh (so
that you can be lovely
again).

103 Cut carefully around
the flower: be careful not
to ruin the thin, almost
liquid membrane of its skin.

104 Bubbling
through the light's surface:
the fractal of
the light.

105 The eye of the Orchid
opens: becomes
the space of memory.

106 & culled from
absence,
you still
throw me
at every turn.

107 Skin black with oil &
milk when I
catch you & pin your
wings to the floor.

108 Overlapping petals
folded
like honeycombs:
because
self-creation is like this
(a burial rite).

109 'but then again I
think I just
wanted to become
adept at being
haunted again.'

110 & the shame is
underneath: it is the
context which you disclaim
as kin.

111 I stood for something
like years, waiting
for the unreleased
parachutes to open.

112 A zero was
circled &
scored—Orphic,
isolated,
understood.

113 In a house without
lights, I'll pluck the music from
your marrow, run
the melodies together, pull
the soul from its sheath.

114 Pulled in two directions at
once like a foregone
conclusion: because consciousness,
as if by magic, has
a contrapuntal texture.

115 Petals flawed
with sunlight, fingers
smeared with mud: the gruel
of winter seed
in our bellies.

116 The moon wears
the skin of the sun turned
inside-out (a blue-bottle mouth
so different than dark,
wild roses).

117 I rinsed you clean in the
heavy water (opened
your mouth with hunger).

118 The bones of the missaid poem
were disinterred &
burned for the sake of closure.

119 Melting like salt in a barrel (the
stars)—& no trace
of love: just the
so-called disorder of beauty.

120 Representing lapses from
the ontological order to
the gentleness the unrevealed: this planet,
sleeping through its orbit.

121 The
smallest
thread
is something
silver
still.

122 Like
a single
ship leaving
the fleet,
desolation
must
be something
like
this:

123 Echoes of
light in parallel
with mourning: as if using
the camera to make paintings
in motion.

124 Naked, grasping the margin of the room—
a summer dress at the
ankles: 'because it's so immensely
difficult to be destroyed
every day by this thing that you are
responsible for loving
anyway—because how could
Love love itself?'

125 Your fingers sliding
around, grasping the sunlit
material of shadow (so just be
careful not to evoke the axioms
of beauty as sin).

126 With the same pathos
that the Greeks employed in
self-revelation: 'because
you expect people to see
everything about
you & they never do.'

127 & yet tropes
survive like viruses:
evolve without
essential structure—

128 Lost love: you have
no name, no copy, no
sound—oozing
through the winter grass.

129 Break
your interiority
like morning bread—

130 Like a Phaedra
burning, daylight tapering
into loss (&
was this nourished only as
love?—this motion which
enjoins you with sight (this
motion which sees you).

131 A color disassembled—cut
into black ribbons: an improvised
shyness: a backbone
glued
to the future of touch.

132 Drawn
naked—each repetition signals the
body's confinement: like a jug
of milk, waiting to fall
from the table.

133 Look inside the architecture of
a star: it is sung
backwards, as if in a dream.

134 Waves of
disinterested sound (unburied from another
life).

135 Spring
lightsome, wave through
wave—hair down: lost
in the sonority of the earth.

136 The caesura marks
the late hour
of forgiveness.

137 Poignantly I laid your
body out
in the slim dark—& poignantly,
each day began.

138 Shapes arranged
into the fragility of truth: half-spectral, half-errant.

139 Nude
turned around
in the stairwell—
nothing
is happening
that is not true.

140 Marked
where the soul
leaves through the skin—
untended
wound—
stripped
of its meaning.

141 & you feel so
quiet when
this porous light
rises from
the water.

142 Sparks of gravity
getting you
off the ground.

143 Bruises touched
into rivers &
oceans & no wayfarer marks
the black sun, sunken
into the evening's ooze.

144 In the
middle of a portrait-sitting:
the faded
yellow of the garden more
precarious than your skin: bitterly
deprived of kindness or
care.

145 Probe through
the brain with a poem,
watch it secrete
a cinema of
sleep.

146 It is nothing we admired:
bleached pearl-petals—
atonements on the order of miracles (& you
slept between my thighs,
night after night).

147 Leaves like wild birds—
taking flight.

148 Founded—
or as foundationless as
the rain?—at a deeper level,
language cools inside
of one perfect mould.

149 The April stars—
floating like anemones in
copper pots (& your
letters falling
out of love).

150 Canticle voices—
endlessly
deferred—thematized
as a sexual wound
in the structure
of music.

151 Like a sheet of glass,
about to be
punched through—sepal,
filament, stigma:
imaged.

152 & teeth clenched, a
chimera is born—almost like a
second thought.

153 Lament &
encomium: in a
deeply stratified poem—
consciousness emerges.

154 A gorgeous
disarticulation passes through
the sentence: Orchid, &
time will pare you down.

155 'Because it's a
lie that there's another mind out
there that can run
alongside yours without
losing its breath.'

156 '& why are you
threading yourself through
everyone like a spiritual
needle—except
out of loneliness?'

157 Attis-blood, the wreaths
of violets, potsherds
altering the salience of
your skin (& so
much is lost
in the witness of devotion).

158 Assured, in
your probation, that
the soul
is a structure of forgetting.

159 You were playing
draughts with
the moon when I found you &
asked you to follow me
wherever I was going.

160 Covered you in linen, indicated
the spot where the
waters would return: sang
the whole earth
into an effigy of ordinary love.

161 Almond-eyes, brutal
in the act of leaving.

162 Sweet, the
grieving rain
punished into life.

163 A lyric startles suddenly,
like a bird,
from the palm of your hand.

164 Clues
scattered across
the matrices
of voice.

165 Why was I not,
in any light,
going back?—touring
the landscape of
ferocious loss?

166 Propositions dense
with metaphor: scripts &
lexicons turned away
from what you learned
by heart.

167 Written like in
a previous book: buried
in the images of the
far interior (an elegy
for the elegy that is yet
unwritten).

168 Because
what is
inexpressible you
forgive: the immense
distance of
a little time.

169 An external object
hidden inside the Orchid?—
like an aria inside
the ear (a soul maybe: beginning
to grow).

170 Dead still inside the
cylinder of the brain: admiring
the privacy of emotions.

171 Asking only for
the return of the ships which disembarked
in the morning of mourning.

172 No—but
a process continues
beyond the margin of the
first person singular—&
you were looking back from
the eye's shyness (& I
saw you).

173 Alert to the grace of
emergence & the sorrow
that enables the thought
to think itself.

174 So the eye
digests the
aesthetics
burrowed inside
of language.

175 The presence of
disquiet is
an estimate of pain: networked—
spread across
you like
lovers on the floor.

176 Blind at the frontier
of an unaccounted-for
fate: only you
may describe this arrival.

177 Translating Time into
the presence
of singular objects (&
the flowers may last two to
three months after which the Orchid
will need to conserve energy for
further leaf bud &
root development).

178 A shared node,
an elliptical
memory: transparent—
shining.

179 So let this book
be a recitation: a remembering
of the love that has always run parallel to me—
as a part of me & as
a part of some other
as-of-yet unfulfilled debt
of grief—so
let this elegy begin.

Lo

[Phrenes Theater Company 2019]
a dramatic text

CHARACTERS:
Lo
Lotus
Locus

SETTING:
A bare stage.

MUSIC:
Permissible with author's permission.

NOTE ON DIALOGUE:
Dialogue is not directed between characters as in a traditional drama but should be rapidly declaimed. In order to indicate and maintain the rhythm, pace, and integrity of declamation, the dialogue will appear in a single stream of verse with an alternative method of signifying who is speaking:

Dialogue in plain lower case is spoken by Lo.
Words in italics lowercase are spoken by Lotus.
WORDS IN PLAIN UPPERCASE ARE SPOKEN BY LOCUS.
* indicates a pause, the span of a few deep breaths.

SCENE 1

Lo and Lotus are alone on the stage.

from a flower sewn in the waste
a tree I grew it and I was reminded
of the cartwheel galaxies
the person I was
abandoned in the dark like old Gloucester
his eyes put out
half
transformed
in a desolate heaven
so I wrote my mother a letter
told her it's just terrible the way time
falls gentle as the rain
it's nearly seven in the
evening now
still cold this late in May
thought about having a child
what that would
would mean now
under
the auspice of elegy
whispering
among
my grandmother's friends
old women in soft nightgowns
straining to hear another
deaf blind dumb
I'm still immature
being a fragment-person
an over-networked over-social person
I think about these things
wonder if I've
finished burning too
without having

started
if the weaving footpaths
lead nowhere in memory except back
to the places they began
or if innocence is really
as tragic as it seems
or if I can penetrate
these meaningless daydreams
a strip of bleached
ground where time has passed

*

walking towards the sea
waves discarded on the shore
like used books
a hopeless desert in the sky
so I pushed the lotus petals
like crumbs from my eyelids
and they denied me water
no
I denied myself
walked
then crawled
until the sun died
and we called it night
a soul
a pearl
clasped between my teeth
I opened my mouth
begged you please
the pearl fell
out
you said nothing
hungry
I abolished
you from sight

just wanting just to be touched
just once

*

tenderly
I resuscitate the dead
at the end of time
when the sky's
the color of confusion

*

fallen ill it's the fault
of the surgery
not being able to have children
fertility means only one thing really
letting nature pass
through
the closed rose of the soul

*

in ten years at the midpoint
of the constellation of your
life you'll have let all this go
like a shadow on a sundial
the absence of light marks
the movement of a circle
I'm not emotionally
involved with anyone
especially myself
can't sleep very well get up to check
my phone
pretend to be cheerful
around people
pretend to feel alive

*

oh please
he said the word pussy

wanted to eat one
mine!
mine!
so I gazed as a stranger
fell low
waiting
like an ember
seducing the sun
drawing it close
then apart
we were together
in the footlights
fell asleep like shadows on the wall
pieces of silk connected
by threads of light
images on a phone
failing to be close
like in a movie
I know I should change my
life but I distrust it
I need to test my
emotions first
so that I can fake them
later
it's like hearing silence
hearing
nothing while listening closely
there's no God he said
and I believed him
because he said it with such
self-possession that it had
to be true
these
delicate nerves
build themselves
build the soul's wings
fly the soul in figure eights

*

he thumbed my pages
read through me
acted on me
like a poison
back broken
I wept I
was ashamed
because let's be
honest I've been living
through my friends
lying
about it afterwards
sex is a part of it
these shards of emotional glass
that pierce my hands
which feel cold
like they've been held to ice
maybe I'm ill again or maybe
it's hypochondria or both
everything that happens is inexplicable
and remains that way
because life is a mood
appearing from nowhere
like a bird from tall grass
it falls
low
falls out
of sight

*

last year
he said
I was a harbor
a sanctuary
the creep

he said my face was like a face
on a book-jacket
just like yours
I said
but the question is always
are you in pain?
are you sorry?
no no no
I'm glad he's gone
he didn't get me
I was his broken toy
tattered white silk
a metaphor for soul-material
very ill
had a fever every night
would touch
myself until I came
I waited
cut myself loose
started floating
hoping to slip beyond
the atmosphere

*

we've been
repeating ourselves
the same words
implying a process
or change
an aesthetics of life
a joke
yet here the blossom lies
inside a mirror
humming
I saw myself looking ruined
and old

120

and meaningless
dead trees brushed with rust
there was music in a cafe
once
a woman played guitar
left her notebook behind
I could not return it
so I read it
memorized her skin
her rose colored eyes
I put my voice in a box
locked that voice inside
muscles constricted
my back shattered
I hobbled
looking for water
I am two things at once
present
in memory
and past in time

*

looking back on who I was
having experienced the
spring in the falling-apart
house with a leaky roof
someone loved me once
too long ago
so there's this sense of wanting now
this bittersweet pang
wanting not unrelated to pain
or the life a worm has
under a log
or a rock
in a garden
remember you said

I believe in nobody
you said this while
I looked in the mirror
I was so unhappy
I projected
onto you
I'm sorry
is the cat
hungry?
a year has passed
just like that

*

I don't think
people will
be people
for too much longer
it seems like there's no need for it now
it's inefficient
in a few more years and
I can confidently detach
spoil myself with the pleasures
of an automated age
dream of disguising myself
leading the other half of my soul to the sea
two desolate figures on a long walk
two voices
rites of rebirth

*

find a target
aim
pulls back the bow
release
my tea's grown cold
my brother calls
complains about being so handsome

no no no
can't get a job I like
barely tolerated the winter
waned spiritually
slipped away
amoeba-like
pathetic
small
a single blinking light
supercharged with fear and pain
lost
inside of self-judgement
I've been brained
like a pig gaping in the slaughteryard
even so I hold
my life like water
inherit a kingdom of smiles
in the upscale supermarket downtown
morning of coffee
lingers on the cortex
I hobble along
open my legs to the first person I meet

*

the earth is in love with the rain
Euripides says
and maybe
we all are
in love
or something like it

*

exfoliation
of forces
energes dynamics economics processes
governing everything
that was formerly

human
governing the body
we can only infer what
an infant feels because
they can't tell us
and so they
are like the dead
not speaking
buried under our care
our talk
our *myths*
I attach my identity to someone
but it fails to hold

*

asking to be devoured
on my knees
numbing the reality of
this wound
the disjunction of selves
at the center of speech
I'll build a tower
conceal myself
protect evasion from truth
my body is occupied
by bodies
tangled up
with a tapestry of symbols
dreams
miseries
back broken
fucked all night and day
I felt like a fool
forgot his name
he had no secrets
was boring

self-involved
a catastrophe
someone who'd quit the world
anxious
like
the rain itself or
the slow shimmering sound of the tea-kettle
after sex
a network of associations
I've erred in trusting others
got dragged down
was seduced by power
lungs bladder intestines blood bones infected ill
it's an unnatural process of
healing hearing
oneself speak
increasing the voltage between hemispheres
losing a little allure each day
seeing younger women
live
in the neighborhoods you once lived in
these are the material facts
these are the moods
like what your mother
said when she was
dying of cancer
I need sleep so
badly but no
one sleeps anymore
this seems to me the
tidal pattern each
of us live
and die by
outside my window
the trees sway and
the leaves are driven

like soldiers back
and forth
across the grass

*

I miss praying
just praying
the way small children pray

*

then
last April you called
told me I was
malleable that I could
change give up smoking
the seduction of images
you blind and me witless
wreaths of wilted grass
in my hair
tugging on my floral miniskirt
with one hand
touching the
scar
on my throat
I wonder whether
I'm still in love with him
with X
because despite myself I would
do it all over again
I don't care if
were if we're monogamous
anymore
just keep me close

*

promote fertility hasten the new birth
burn the pine trees in the autumn

adorn the altar with violets
it's the possibility of helping him grow
that obsesses me
which is stupid but
our respective neuroses make
it so comfortable to
spend weekends together
I'm fond of him
he's simple and so
hurt even though he's
almost forty
still works out every day eats well
drinks moderately has a good job
doesn't give a fuck about art or ideas
thinks he's smarter than me
doesn't ask for sex too much
doesn't ask enough
expects me to ask
a part of him hates me
thinks I'm an unhappy disconnected woman
which I am
I wonder if we are all incarnations
of the ancient dead
souls
in the bodies of birds
seeding the clouds for rain
preparing the earth
for spring
I wonder

*

burn the effigy
of pain
uncertainty
pick
fresh mountain flowers
from the wounds of my eyes

*

a secret
a disorganized notion of continuity
the soul does not hesitate
to lie or disassemble
manic
misdirected self-love
goes nowhere

*

a winter sun in tatters
a beautiful lifeless doll
very good at playing the victim
put my eyes out
like Oedipus
at six o'clock the work day ends
in theory
most of us remain
buried alive

*

when I think about 'fucking
for real' penetrating
and especially being
penetrated by people
I feel preemptive exhaustion
over the phone I said
that marriage is a certain way of
solving our problem
I guess I meant it
it's nonsense
the houses are so pretty here
close to the sea
found a symbol in myself
split in two
love is
devotion

to the great need to
discover Dharma
or duty
or something
how loathsome old people are
I'm cut
into images like ribbons
cameras create sorrow
converts us
into data
lie to us
yet how can you know
a woman is experiencing pleasure
she may be faking it

SCENE 2
Enter Locus.

shadow
of memory
THE RECENTLY
dead
LIKE PILOTS
flying in circles
the brain's hemispheres
THE LOCUS OF CONTROL
what people pretend is true
DESIRE
eroticism
as if we were
REAL
we're not
RETAIN THE CHORUS LEAVE
the tragedy behind
Narcissus flowers
Narcissus soul

*

LOOK
a stain on the bed
MY STAIN
no one else's
kiss me wind my hair with wind
don't be indifferent
SOFTLY
apply pressure
USE MY LANGUAGE
let me use
yours
LIKE
the migration of birds

*

nothing is alive
these poems
our voices
HOLLOW
a simple pattern
of increasing
COMPLEXITY
speak a picture of the heart
sculpt it
APPLE-WHITE
in the evening sun
half-naked drunk enough
BETRAY A SECRET
make a myth
so again it's you

*

quick loops of breath
SADNESS SEEPS
in
ruins the blue enamel
OF THE SKY
pear trees a garden wall
A CHILD SCAMPERING
across the grass
WE'RE HERE
in the quiet
montage of emotional shocks
THE BIRDS RETURN
with spring arriving
I BEGIN
just begin
anywhere

*

photographs of me
REVEAL
a startling hunger

*

go to social gatherings of disparate
individuals who seem
to have little in common
EMOTIONALLY DISFIGURED PEOPLE
deeply isolated and lonely

*

scatter the fragments of my eyes
sew me sing me into the earth
CARRY THE IMAGE AWAY
my throat cut
IN TIME FOR SPRING
the procession goes through the streets of the village
I am all of them at once
the girls going from house to house
SINGING
"beautiful death"

*

in the fields
where we buried ourselves
AT A CROSSROADS
uprooted
forgotten
ABSENT
but how long
have we waited?

*

a young virgin thrown
in the river
THE BODY OF THE CORN-GOD
severed

the first sheaves of corn
cut
CHANTING
goddess I've
NEVER RECEIVED A LOVE LETTER
until I
went home with someone I hated last night
blew him he
HAD EYES LIKE A LITTLE BOY'S
for fuck's sake
slept through my alarm missed work
TEXTED MY SISTER WONDERING
if I was falling apart
perpetually haunted
BY FAILED POTENTIAL
the failure to love anyone more
than myself

*

READING THE VEDAS
hoping for a spiritual shock
because the summer's always ending
LIKE WHEN YOU WERE A KID
school's always starting the fun's
ALWAYS ALMOST OVER

*

HEART
dry as bone
sleep schedule a mess
NOBODY KNOWS
nobody cares
he was depressed yesterday said
he hates birthdays it wasn't my fault
I TOLD HIM TO GO
couldn't say what was on my mind
hushed after dinner got

TOO DRUNK
he's avoiding marriage
but so am I
extraordinarily naive
he's featureless self-absorbed
BUT MAYBE I AM TOO
I worry about that
ABOUT MYSELF
we never talk about the mundane embarrassing aspects
of our lives
WE ACT
as if we'll live forever

*

from a flower sewn in the waste
shades drawn
IN AN EMPTY HOUSE
at fifteen alone for the first time
touching secretly
the senses alive
LIKE NEON LIGHTS
eyes
BURIED
at twilight
the body turned to water

*

the love behind the heart
LIKE LIGHT THROUGH A SCREEN
the lies I've
TOLD
too many books too
little furniture no clutter
HIS APARTMENT
anxious
FROM AN OBLIQUE ANGLE
eyes in my feet

trampling the sunlight
the body falls apart it doesn't matter
how old you are
IT HAPPENS
it's a bitter thing
life for life's sake
JUST AS IT IS
there's no starting over
I won't call him tomorrow
even though
I WAS UNFAIR TO HIM
but it doesn't matter
LOOK!
the sky crooked with fire

*

PHRASES
and
sentences
ARE SUPER CONNECTIVE
divide like cells
syntax loosens
LIKE A BELT
around
the waist
first things first
THE SUN CLOTHED
in the eye's cloth
the
LIGHT
shuffled
like a pack of cards
ALL
these symbols
like
RINGS AROUND
a tree

*

I MADE
my own heart
slowly
like the sign
of the cross
SET
the table
pour the wine
CARRY ME
across
the threshold of names
SOUNDS
signs
please
hit me across the mouth
make me
SMILE
our words
have unregulated
POWER

*

PIANO-SHADOWS
and trees in the
dusk
MY GRANDFATHER FATHER WAS
sick and bruised easily
because of the medication

*

translucent
PERMEABLE
the coronal darkness
round the sun
LIKE
a Rembrandt

the taste of cardamom
today before
YOU WENT TO WORK
each of us
talked about
the sincerity
WE DID NOT ASK FOR
simple days
our meek habits
DON'T
acknowledge
the fluoride in the water
DON'T
acknowledge
our stained teeth

*

with one wing
twisted
LIKE THE SHAPE
of hunger
death
IS ONE OF THOSE THINGS
a body goes through
IT'S
something
YOU
can taste
like lemon in tea

*

pried open
LIKE A CAN
a
STRESS
on the syllables of
disappointment

spring
slashed open
winter's throat
but
YOU COULD SING
every bit of me
back into hope

*

images
leak
back into
THE BRAIN OPEN
the archive
of beauty
LOOK INSIDE
because
beauty
IS
the source of itself

*

do the birds
OBSERVE ME?
walking
ACROSS
the park
to work
the way
I WATCH THEM?

*

rainflower
let the solstice
ENTER
through
THE UNHEALED

heart
of the eye

*

LOOK
look
look!

Field of Trembling

[2019. Text for performance, originated by Emily Gasda]
[TornPage, NYC]

I live in a room with white curtains
Wooden floors
Linen sheets
And two dresses
With a glass on the table
Like a husband
Or an animal
Now I live alone
In a room with white curtains
It blurs
Hats with feathers
Footpaths dark with rain
Waiting for the trolley
A sketch of the city
Very beautiful
But what do I mean?
Art in accord with nature
But how?
This is the hour when the hands speak
With the fingers of language I shape you
No one may know what you're feeling
A radical new way of seeing
In a room with white curtains
Move the easel to catch the light
Sudden memories of girlhood
A noise woke me up this morning
And everything was swollen throbbing
I'd been dreaming of a symphony
In silence I sat and listened
An orchestra on stage but no music
Just images on a screen
Like at the picture show

The images draw close to me
I don't draw them at all
Like animals creeping close to a fire
I feed them by hand
Night by night I tame them
Until they accept captivity
They stay beside and protect me

*

A body has one voice with one tone
The voice ages
It gets lower or higher
Softer or louder
Angriero
More loving
But there is no shift of the inner truth
You discover in your training only fate
Always within
Always waiting
The oak in the acorn
A new woman
An emancipated woman
A woman artist
All names for me
To which I am indifferent
My limbs are heavy
Even with twelve hours of rest
I have no more interest in stillness
But how do I wake?
The days are getting shorter
My room is getting colder
I heard that Russians come to Europe
And can't believe our windows have no double panes
That I live in the most modern city in the world
But my feet are cold
And my hands turn blue in November

I just want to sleep
And feel my head spin
And my eyes roll back
But I should light the stove and read
The subject hums with fructifying life
While I stand aside and wait
Holes are made in the fence
That separates my mind
From the chaos around it
As if night could leak through
The barrier of day's blue
Sticky to the touch

*

I had to leave the colony
I was too strong and they were too weak
Strength is holy
And the soul the fruit of the body's labors
Like cornmeal
Ground like kernels of the sun
And baked in the night
In the grove of Demeter
Where I await
Arranging sticks into a topiary
Hold out your holy oak and your laughter
By spring I will join you
Let my body grow ripe again
Sweet again
Magnificent pine trees
I call them my men
Thick
Gnarled
Powerful
Tall
Yet delicate nerves and fibers in them
Birch trees

Delicate and slender and young
Delight with that relaxed and dreamy face
As if life for them has not really begun
Willows
With your knotted trunks
You're my old men
I have company enough
I do
And it's my own company
We understand each other well
And then a human life
Is like a forest clearing
A gap opens
The forest closes around it
And maybe it was never there
No God
No guide
Alone but not abandoned
For I have not abandoned myself
When the silence on the fringe overcomes me
I talk

*

In Berlin
Four floors above the street
I can't see much of the sky
Beneath me from the courtyard
I hear the thumping of a woman
Beating the dust from her rug
I live a strange life here
As if possessed
Neither here nor there
I feel waves of slow horror come over me
But they are less than they had been
He comes to mind
He writes like someone

Crying out in their sleep
I left last autumn
Before I returned
This autumn I left for good
And he calls me
I call him nothing
I wish to forget
Another attack of despondency
Write me back right away
Come visit the city this autumn
We'll walk along the canals
Rejoice in the gold and black hues
Or in winter see the holly hung in clusters
Along the river's limpid blue
You came and talked about Russia
You told me what it was like
You met Tolstoy with his long white beard
You said he has the feet of a girl
Small and fine
You posted a packet
Of the sketchbooks I left behind
You wrote me as well:
The work is good
What does he know?
I face obstacles in my work
Obstacles he can't grasp
In the colony I was still with him
My husband
A bohemian life in a loose dress
That wasn't good enough
Not as long as I was in his bed
It was not enough
He finds no joy in progress
He laments
He builds windows
Traced with dust and rain

So that the muddy light of longing
Can fill up the room
He never goes into
If I knew that place
I would leave
If you knew that place
You would remain
Content with local fame
But solipsism
When is it a guiding hand
And when is it the end?
Well, a man may stand there, loitering
A woman
Associated with concession
Must erase herself from her work
Condemned to witness death
Over and over again
Haunting shifts of perspective
Voices from the world outside
Pity like terror is activated
Then set aside
We're alive on the same earth
I stretch my hand out from afar
For love and forgiveness are the same
Spring dies all the way through the fall
The harvest slips through my hands
I spread honey on the black of the earth
And must find a way forward without him
Though I bleed and my guts trail behind me
On a grotesque path to the summer
I was so unconscious
Wanting to create life
Wanting him to make it conscious
But now I've made it conscious myself
And the extreme pressure has lifted
And it can happen at any time

I have money enough to live this way for a year
To live my childhood again at my own will
I'm not guilty of any childhood crimes
I can put that behind me now

*

The more you eliminate the ethical viewpoint
The more you come to a style
Is that a true education?
Whipping the human beast
Until in ecstasy it collapses?
Where does this leave the beautiful things?
What of that which isn't superhuman?
We were arguing about this at the cafe
Reflected in the mirrored walls
Under the light of chandeliers
It all felt alien to me
But wonderful too
The year began thus
In fur and gold
In rings of smoke
The birds flew from our noise
Ahead and above
Below and behind
All around the piano we sat
Singing Schubert's Allmacht
I sang more there
In the dense wood behind the house
Where I knew every hedge
This is the one regret left

*

The imagination doubles reality
Somehow makes it more concrete
Paintings being emblems
Of the mind's estrangement from the world
A month ago I was so sure

Now I stand a beggar pleading in the cold
Do you know when the work inside you
Is no longer there to be expressed?
You feel afloat for a reason
Nothing moors you
No one seeks you
It's a violent form of idleness
That leaves the world without a trace of itself
Without representation
But I may perform a desperate cry
For respite from myself
For the first time
What I make I could love
The five doors of beauty shut
And the weight of lightness
Settles into the fatal dignity of form
And the previous day shrinks
And takes the shape of a cut flower
In a blue glazed vase
I meditate on Ariadne's thread
In a trance
Following the unrolling of the yarn
And the joy I feel is very deep
For all of this suffering
Is to be joined with you
The seed of experience
Remains alive overnight
In the ether of death and sleep
For another chance to be exhausted by day
To grow
To be cut
To be placed in the vase

*

A saint in Hildegard's age
Could count every soul they knew one by one

And believed every soul might be saved
You never left the earth
And the earth never left you
Today there are more souls than you can count
So you begin to doubt
That they can be saved
The story of this century
Will be the loss of craft to the machine
We are the impotent allies of the machines we build
Slaves of the fate we mean to master
There's a department store with sixty-five escalators
Carrying people like letters through pneumatic tubes
We need little sleep
And are never tired
There is very little of the future left
It has all arrived
At night I smell the cars
And it mixes so strangely with the other smells
But I've chosen to be here
In the vital nerve of this new world
Curiosity supersedes disgust
In the disappearance of old ways and means of being
Possibility appears
Will I carry it out?
But give me something real
Something, anything
But not choice
If you can choose
It means nothing

*

Am I ready to love?
I saw my family and they asked me that
Can't I love anyone else?
I don't think my father agrees
I showed them the painting of the woods

Birch trees by the lake
They must prefer an old forest of maple and oak
They said nothing
So I have taken stock of the world of my childhood
And found it wanting
Nothing but manners
Manners of repression
Comfort in diffidence
When what has begun to expand shrinks back
And never diffuses again
Making it impossible
To strive towards unity in anything
And I can only forgive them
For bringing me into the world
When they themselves were children
My childhood I encounter everywhere
In contemplation of the countless façades of the city
A front door in the old West End
Was this mine?
Is this the place I was born with my brothers and my sisters?
Stained glass windows
I feel like my eyes are stained glass windows
It's always sunset and dawn
But take comfort
I may live well and die old
I may live well and die young
I may close my eyes and not live at all
I may close my eyes
I may live
I may die
And here by the stove it's warm
There is nowhere left to go anyway
I'm here again, living
Watching the years rise to the top of the pile and fall off
Half the morning mustering the courage to mail a letter
You must understand how I have plumbed the depths

I need to hear that you know what I have done
The desire to be seen erects a barrier
Between myself and the world
As irreversible as an edict of the divine
And renders me invisible

*

Figures seated around a cafe table
A charcoal drawing
Hurried
They don't notice me
I have always tried
To share in friendships with men
But their darkness is murky
And specific to them
And flows into the river of neglect
Against its own reason
Against its own purpose
And I've always been rebuffed
Held at arm's length
I can't know the rhythm
I can't know the song
They stop my ears
Except you
That's the one thing you didn't do
Sometimes I dream of going to a brothel
With my hair under a cap
And having my way
Having my way
Having my way
No society is free of habitual cruelty
A civilization achieves success
When it diverts and diffuses its pathologies
But I just want a place on earth
Before it all comes to an end
While a peaceful existence is possible

I see the dewy gossamer threads
And I'm careful not to break them
I can follow them somewhere
Extend them
Draw a line
Cut it in half
And you can continue an infinite number of times
In this way, life might be said to be eternal
The last moment can always be divided further

*

Help me
I am lost
We must be two not one
I say that to the one who is far away
We must be two not one
I close my eyes
Over and over again
I repent and I repent
With an urgent wound
I'll sit with you
And make peace with what's disappeared
Walking through a crowded arcade
Shafts of sunlight break into pieces on the ground
We're leaving the studio of renown
You try to take my hand and I walk ahead
I remember this to release it
But it only creates bottomless grief
I can't recall what it was
I can't recall
The shadow of a loss
My flesh and blood
Shoals and sandbars
Mud flats and empty straits
The stench of the stagnant harbor
The heat of the sun

Fear it no more
From endless space
From heights and depths come the sounds of birds
Teeu teeu
Vow vow vow
Kaitch kaitch kaitch

*

Snow
The year is almost over
Dawn is creeping up
Perhaps I'm in a quiescence
My senses are rearranging
I need not do anything but rest
What of my dream
That I was on a night train to Zittau
On the border of Bohemia
I had been there years ago
To the field of trembling
But the train never arrived in the dream
It was snowing too
Like the spell I was under
When I first arrived here
Was sweet, so sweet
But only a dream
And one that couldn't last long
For the reaction had to come
Then something truer
Serious work and serious living
In between utter formlessness
A battle I fight tooth and nail
To dissipate and not know
How to capture myself again
But something will break through
And make me greater than I had been
What stirs is but a flicker of hope

To exist outside as in ourselves
I the fool
May see the flame licking at the dark
And try to grab the candle
And find my own nose
And look down at my fingers
And take a step backward out of confusion
And tumble to the floor
And either laugh or cry
But in this second year of the century
This is the year
I will become a woman of grace.

CPSIA information can be obtained
at www.ICGtesting.com
Printed in the USA
BVHW041706170523
664362BV00004B/206